Take A Number

New ideas
+ imagination =
more fun

Jeanne Bendick
Marcia Levin
pictures by Jeanne Bendick

Whittlesey House · McGraw-Hill
New York · Toronto · London

many thanks

to all the people who helped with this book:

to Leonard Simon, Junior High School Curriculum Co-ordinator, for his splendid suggestions and equal patience,

to John Techet of the Ridge Street School, Town of Rye,

to David Pugh, who was a conscientious critic,

and to David Pinkham, Woody Struthers, Hugh Levin, Nandra Siwek, and Theresa Donahue, who all helped too.

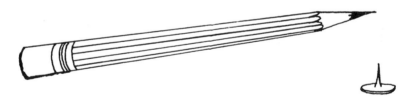

TAKE A NUMBER

Copyright © 1961 by Jeanne Bendick and Marcia O. Levin. All rights reserved. This book or parts thereof may not be reproduced in any form without written permission of the publishers.
Printed in the United States of America.
Library of Congress Catalog Card Number: 61–12034
Published by Whittlesey House, a division of the McGraw-Hill Book Company, Inc.
04483
Fourth Printing

contents

37

WHAT IS A NUMBER?

What is a number?
What does "number" mean to you?
Think about any number—perhaps the number 7.
What does 7 mean to you?
How did we get the idea of 7?
Could we say that a set of 7 children

is like a set of 7 clouds?

or a set of 7 cups?

Seven cups and seven clouds and seven children are not all things you can touch or hear or hold. They're not all big or little or black or white, but all these sets are alike in one way. They each contain the same number of things, 7.

4

7 *always* means this many things | | | | | | |
no matter what they are.

They don't even have to be the same kind of things.
Put seven things on a bare table top.   Maybe you put

2 gloves
3 books
1 key
1 cookie
on the table.

They are not alike.   But you have
a set of 7 things on the table.

We can talk about:
2 sneakers
1 mouse
3 stars   and
1 idea
and we have talked about 7 things,
because 7 *always* stands for the same
number.

2 *always* means this many things | |
600 *always* means a definite number of things
and so does 1,000,000.

At first people thought you could only count *things*, and
that you couldn't have numbers without having the things
to which they belonged.

In fact, the way they learned to count was by matching
things—

fingers with arrowheads
pebbles with sheep
marks with members of a tribe

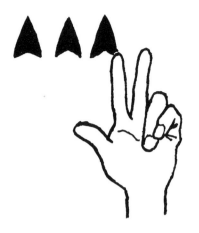

A primitive man put up a finger for each arrowhead, and he could see when the number of fingers he raised was the same as the number of arrowheads. So he really didn't have to have a name, like "three" for a number. He counted by matching.

You match things all the time.

You set a place and a chair for each person at the dinner table.

If you are serving soda to your friends, you have a bottle for each one.

If you are playing a tennis game, you have a racquet for each player.

Mathematicians give this way of matching a special name. They call it a "one-to-one correspondence," and it is an important step in learning about numbers. You can see that one arrowhead is matched with one finger, and one sodapop is matched with one friend.

When men were first learning to count by matching, they did not have names for each number.

We are so used to "one, two, three," that we hardly ever stop to think that someone had to make up those number names. In French, their names are "un, deux, trois." In German they are "eins, zwei, drei." Maybe in cave language they were "oof, ba, ik." The number names aren't really important. But whatever the names are, in any language, the same name has to stand for the same number at all times.

1	2	3
one	two	three
un	deux	trois
ein	zwei	drei
oof	ba	ik

The name of a number is its *numeral.*

You use a numeral to talk about a number.

You use the name of a number—its numeral—the way you use the name of a person or a thing.

Did you have this to eat today?

Of course you didn't eat the word "candy" today, but you know what the word stands for. You ate what the word stands for. The word "candy" is the symbol for the thing that you ate.

Did you use this today?

You know that "7" stands for 7 somethings.

The number symbol you write is the symbol for the idea of 7 somethings. What is on the blackboard is the name or the numeral that stands for the *idea* of 7.

You can't put the 7 things on the board, any more than you can put the actual candy on the board.

But the numeral "7" stands for the idea of 7 just as the word "candy" stands for the idea of candy.

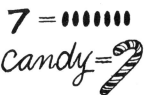

$7 = $ ❘❘❘❘❘❘❘

candy =

Numbers are exact. Seven always means *exactly* seven. Nine always means *exactly* nine, not a little more or a little less.

Words are not nearly so exact as numbers. If you write, "A fat and smiling man in a fuzzy suit," everyone who reads the words will imagine the man in his own way. No matter how many extra words you use to describe the man, each reader will see something a little different in his mind.

But right from the beginning, people understood that 3 fish were *always* 3—not 2½ or 3¼, but *exactly* 3.

They also learned that two was one more than one.

And if you added one more you always got 3, which is 1 and 1 and 1. Each number was one more than the number before it. So they began to see an order in counting, and mathematical thinking began.

$$\text{\Large A} + \text{\Large A} = \text{\Large AA} + \text{\Large A} = \text{\Large AAA}$$
$$1 \quad\; 1 \quad\;\; 2 \quad\; 1 \quad\;\;\;\; 3$$

You can count almost anything as long as you have a place to start and a way of putting the things you are counting in order, so you can think about them one at a time. This means that you are arranging them, either really or in your mind, so that only one numeral stands for each thing you want to count.

Probably the early number names only went up to five for the five fingers on one hand, which was a very useful counting tool. There are people in the world today who don't count any higher. And there are people to whom twenty, or all their fingers and toes, is the highest number. In the language of one Indian tribe in a remote part of South America, the words,

one hand mean 5
two hands mean 10
two hands and a foot mean 15, and
both hands and feet mean 20.

So, at first, three, or five, or twenty were very big numbers. But they were not big enough.

Suppose a shepherd had to count a very large flock of sheep. How could he do it?

He might use a little pebble to stand for each sheep until he counted 10, then put a bigger stone aside to stand for each *group of 10*. When he finished, he'd know that each stone stood for 10 sheep and each pebble stood for one sheep, and he could count the total faster than if he just had many, many pebbles.

You do the same thing when you change 10 pennies for a dime. It is certainly easier to count 10 dimes than 100 pennies. You know they are both worth a dollar, but fewer pieces of money (or fewer numbers) are easier to work with.

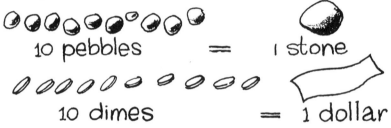

10 pebbles = 1 stone

10 dimes = 1 dollar

Someone thought of putting notches or marks on a stick. Maybe he crossed off four strokes with a fifth stroke—like this: ‖‖‖. Maybe he used a bigger notch to stand for a group, the way the shepherd used a bigger pebble.

Then he counted the groups. You sometimes keep score in games that way today. You just have to count the groups and the number of strokes left over to know what your score is.

Later, when people got used to bigger numbers, they made a row of ten marks with a cross through them to stand for 10, like this:

10

Soon they were just using the X for ten, and they only had to count the "X's." Years later, the Romans were still using the "X" as their symbol for ten. You may see it today on some clocks or as a chapter heading in a book.

It took many, many years for counting to develop to the "grouping" stage. But now men needed more kinds of numbers and better ways of using them, because they were doing more difficult things than counting arrows or sheep. They were trading with each other, building houses, dividing fields, and even paying taxes. As life became more complicated, people had to write numerals for large and small numbers, and write them so that other people could read them and understand what they meant.

Just think of a world without numbers! It would be difficult to know how old you are, how much you weigh, or how tall you are.

You wouldn't have money, or be able to tell what time it was, or the day of the month.

It would be hard to know the distance from one place to another.

Without numbers men could never have built ships or cities, or explored the seas, or taken their first steps to the stars.

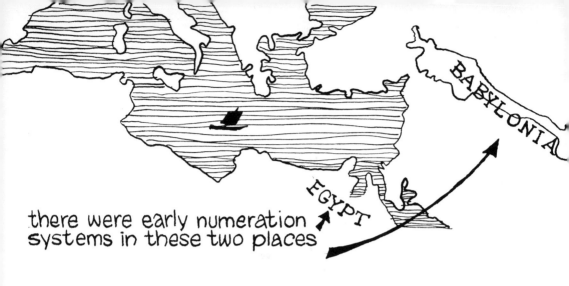

there were early numeration systems in these two places

THE FIRST NUMERATION SYSTEMS

When we have a collection of number symbols and a plan for writing these symbols to express our number ideas, we say we have a *system of numeration.*

Let's look at two systems of numeration that were used about 5,000 years ago. It is surprising how much alike they were, because the people who used them lived very far apart.

In Egypt the numerals were written in ink on papyrus, which was made from the stem of a plant. (Where do you think our word "paper" came from?)

They looked like this:

1	2	3	4	5	6	7	8	9	10	11	100
I	II	III	IIII	III II	III III	IIII III	IIII IIII	III III III	∩	∩I	ℓ

Early Egyptian numerals are not hard for us to read.

Strokes were used for the numbers from one to nine, then a new symbol for ten.

Then they combined the symbols for one and ten to make eleven, ∩I

and two and ten to make twelve— ∩II

and so on.

The Babylonians wrote their numerals on soft clay, so the strokes were shaped a little differently. But the systems were much the same.

Υ	ΥΥ	ΥΥΥ	ΥΥΥΥ	ΥΥΥ ΥΥ	ΥΥΥ ΥΥΥ	ΥΥΥΥ ΥΥΥ	ΥΥΥΥ ΥΥΥΥ	ΥΥΥΥΥ ΥΥΥΥ	<	<Υ	Υ
1	2	3	4	5	6	7	8	9	10	11	60

Can you see one important difference between the Egyptian and the Babylonian systems?

The Egyptians used combinations of strokes and the "10" sign until they got to 99, which looked like this: ∩∩∩∩∩ ⫼ ∩∩∩∩ ⫼ ⫼ and then they made a new symbol for 100: ℓ

The Babylonians used the sign for 10 only until they got to 59: <<< ΥΥΥΥΥ << ΥΥΥΥ and then they made a new sign for 60: Υ

The Egyptian system had a *base* of ten. The Babylonian numeration system had a *base* of sixty.

The Roman System

Many years after the Babylonians and the Egyptians, the Romans developed their own numeration system.

The Romans had a great civilization. They built wonderful aqueducts to carry water, and roads which are still used today. They built great cities which had apartment houses with bathrooms and running water. They conquered many countries, started many colonies, and ruled a large empire. They wrote books which are still read and studied.

But the Romans were never able to develop a numeration system that was easy to work with.

Their first three symbols were those same old strokes:

I II III

But instead of making strokes all the way up to ten, the Romans used a special symbol for five— the letter V. Do you think they could have chosen "V" this way?

The Roman numerals looked like this:

I	II	III	IV	V	VI	VII	VIII	IX	X
1	2	3	4	5	6	7	8	9	10
			(5-1)		(5+1)	(5+2)	(5+3)	(10-1)	

Notice how the strokes that are placed to the left of "V" or "X" have a different meaning from the strokes that are placed to the right.

The Romans used letters not only for five and ten, but for larger numbers too.

They used "L" for fifty. (They borrowed the Greek "V" for fifty, and straightened it out.)

Their word for "hundred" was *centum,* so the sign for one hundred was "C."

Their word for "thousand" was *mille,* so one thousand was "M."

The Roman numeration system was used for hundreds of years. It was useful for recording information, but difficult to work problems with.

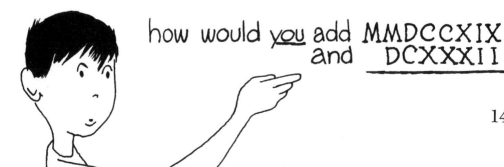

how would you add MMDCCXIX
and DCXXXII

In our numerals we would write and the answer would be simple to find—

$$2719$$
$$\underline{632}$$
$$3351$$

Multiplication was even harder. If we want to multiply 27×16, it looks like this:

$$27$$
$$\times \underline{16}$$
$$162$$
$$\underline{27}$$
$$432$$

But if the Romans had wanted to write the same problem it would have looked like this:

and the final answer would have been **CDXXXII.**

Instead of doing such long and complicated work, they used a device that was a lot like the shepherd's pebbles. It was called an *abacus.*

Does it look like a baby's toy? These number frames are not toys to anyone who has to work with figures. They are the only quick way some people have to add or subtract, multiply or divide.

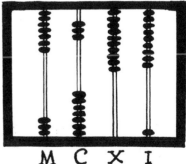

a simple abacus looks like this (some have many more bars and counters)

15

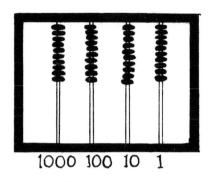

1000 100 10 1

Each bead in the first row at the right was worth one.

Each bead in the second row was worth ten ones, or 10.

Each bead in the third row was worth ten tens, or 100, and so on.

Almost every civilization developed its own form of abacus. The Mexican Indians had abacuses when Columbus came to America. The Egyptians and Chinese had used them thousands of years before that.

Abacuses probably began from the ancient way of counting pebbles. Instead of having to find new pebbles each time, or taking them out of a little bag and then putting them in place, men learned to make counting frames. Holes were pierced in the pebbles so they could be placed on a row of upright sticks, like this:

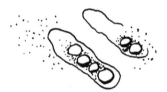

the first abacuses were probably just pebbles in the sand

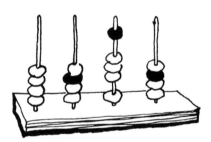

then the pebbles were put on sticks

Finally the frames were enclosed so the pebbles or beads couldn't fall off. Even today, modern Chinese, Japanese, and Russian businessmen often use them for figuring; and they can work as fast as some people can with adding machines.

Can you see why number operations can be done so well on an abacus?

Let's take another look:

There are ten beads on each stick.

Suppose we move two beads down on the first stick to the right. (On closed frames, beads are usually moved from top to bottom.)

You can tell that we are talking about the number two.

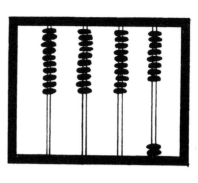

But suppose we move two beads on the stick in the *next* place, like this:

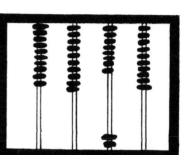

Are we still talking about two? No!

Even though we have only moved two beads, you know we mean *twenty* because we have moved the beads in the tens (two digit) column, or *place*. And if we moved the beads on the next wire, like this:

they would mean two *hundred,* because the beads are in the hundreds *place.*

So 2 (or any number symbol up to and including 9) not only has its actual value,

the actual value of a numeral is the number of things· or numbers· it stands for

2   5

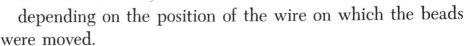

two thousand
two hundred
& twenty two

but it also has a *place value*. It
can stand for two units,
    or two tens,
    or two hundreds,
    or two thousands,
depending on the position of the wire on which the beads
were moved.

1000   100   10   1

In the old ways of writing numerals, there was no such
thing as *place value*. When people needed larger numerals,
they had to make up new symbols for them.

Until quite lately there was almost no connection between
writing numerals and working problems. The problem was
solved on an abacus, and then the answer was written down.
Arithmetic was a long, slow process because *something was
missing*.

Can you figure out what the missing thing was?

Was it a numeral?

But people could count to millions.

Was it a way to do examples?

They knew how to add and subtract, multiply and divide.
They knew how to "carry" and to "borrow."

Was it an *idea* that was missing?
What do you think?

WHAT THE HINDU-ARABIC
SYSTEM GAVE US

If you can't think what the missing thing was right away, don't worry about it. Almost everyone in the world overlooked it until almost 3,500 years after the Babylonians and the Egyptians began to write numerals.

Among the first people to discover the missing thing were the Mayan Indians in South America, but they had no way to pass it on. No one in the civilized world even dreamed that there was land or people on the other side of the western sea.

The part that was so amazing, or so sad, whichever way you want to look at it, was that there had been wonderful number systems in some parts of the world for a long time. But in those days the world seemed very big and people were very far apart. There were no television sets or radios to carry news from one country to another. There were no airplanes, or trains, or fast ships. There weren't even good roads for horses, or camels, or donkeys, so it's no wonder it took so long for knowledge to travel from one place to another.

About 500 years before the Mayans, a wonderful new number system had developed in India. This system had a special, different symbol for every number up to nine.

They looked like this:

९ ૨ ३ ૪ ૫ ६ ७ ८ ૯
1 2 3 4 5 6 7 8 9

This was certainly easier than counting strokes!

But the most exciting part of this system was the *tenth* symbol. It looked like this:

O

We call it *zero*.

What does "zero" mean to you?

How do you start thinking about zero?

But how did people ever manage without zero?

This wonderful symbol "0" makes it possible to write all the whole numbers with just these symbols:

O 1 2 3 4 5 6 7 8 9

Every time we want to write a number larger than nine, we use a combination of two or more of these symbols.

10   261   3487   1000000002

Remember how the Romans showed numbers on the abacus?

What did it mean when they put two beads on different wires? Weren't they showing place value?

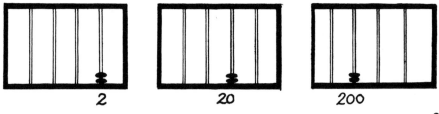

2   20   200

We do the same thing. The zero shows us the place value of the number. And, by just attaching one "0" to a numeral, or two "0's," or as many as you wish, you move a numeral into the next bigger column in your mind, like this:

			2
		2	0
	2	0	0
2	0	0	0

Our numerals give you an abacus right in your head!

When you write "203" it is a fast way of writing, "two hundreds, no tens, three ones." What is "320" a fast way of writing? How would you show 30

or 300 without "0"?

How would you show "705"?

You would need an abacus!

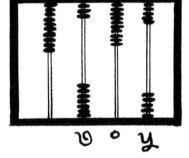

Zero also holds a place where there are no numbers.

Some people think that's how "0" started. It marked an empty rod on the abacus, so no one would make a mistake when he wrote an answer down in symbols.

For the first time in history, zero made it easier to work problems with written symbols than to figure them out with beads.

The Arabs learned this numeration system from the Hindus. They changed the symbols, little by little, until they looked like the "Arabic" numerals we use today.

I 2 3 4 4 6 7 8 9

1 2 3 4 5 6 7 8 9

RULES ABOUT NUMBERS

Numbers aren't very useful without rules. The first people who used numbers found this out.

2 men

1 man

This always had to be one man, and if another stood beside him there were two men. Do you remember we said that whenever you added one to the number before it, you got one more? This is a rule.

When you use place values you are following a rule.

The rules tell you what you can do with numbers and what you can't do. If you don't obey the rules, the numbers are useless.

But did you know that you can make up new rules if you need them? Mathematicians do it all the time. As long as they obey the new rules they set up, the numbers work out right.

All over the world, cars stop at the red light and go on green. That's the rule, and everyone obeys it. But, if, for some reason, we made a new rule, so that everybody stopped on green and went on red, it would work out just as well. The important thing is to know which rule you are following, or there would be a terrible mixup. It is also important for everybody to follow the same rules.

cars stop on red and go on green, but the other way round would work as well

Mathematicians have always made up new rules as they needed them or as they thought of them. Without the new rules they would never have invented zero, or discovered atomic energy, or built computers, or sent satellites into space.

Sometimes the new rules are just a change in the order of doing things. In mathematics this can make a big difference, just as it can when you are cooking or doing a chemistry experiment.

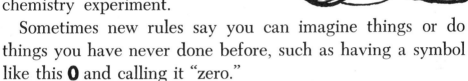

Sometimes new rules say you can imagine things or do things you have never done before, such as having a symbol like this **0** and calling it "zero."

Sometimes there is a whole set of new symbols with new rules about using them.

After you have made up **0**,

if you say that attaching it to a digit, like this, **10**

moves that digit into the tens column, you have made up a new rule.

The Hindus invented a whole set of new symbols.

If you made up two new symbols, ◄►- and ⊔ , and then said that ◄►- + ◄►- = ⊔ , it would be a new rule.

But you have to know a lot about mathematics to make up *important* new rules. You have to know what the old rules are, too, because if you didn't and you tried to make up a new rule that said $1 + 1 = 3$, it would only lead to confusion.

That's one more reason for learning mathematics. The more you know, the easier it is to have fun with it.

1+1=2   1+1=3

BASES FOR THE NUMERALS WE USE

The numeration system that the Hindus invented has a base of ten. We call it a *decimal* system. The Egyptian system and the Roman system had a base of ten, too. The word "decimal" comes from the Latin word "decem," which means "ten." (If you think, then, that December should be the tenth month you are right, and originally it was.)

the Roman months were:

1	2	3	4	5

Martius, Aprilis, Maius, Junius, Quintilis,

6	7	8	9

Sextilis, September, October, November and

10	then they added

December.   Januarius and Februarius

The Babylonian system was based on sixty.

There is that word "base" again!

What do we mean when we say that? What is a *base* for a system of numerals anyway?

A base is just a way of grouping numbers.

We group our numbers into tens,   **10**
then ten times ten, or hundreds, then   **100**
ten times ten times ten, or thousands.   **1000**

Ten is our base. We always come back to a multiple of ten when we count, before we go on, just the way a player goes back to home base.

0 1 2 3 4 5 6 7 8 9

10   11   12

Our numeration system helps us to work out problems.
Look at this:
What has it got to do with base 10?
What part does zero play?

$$\begin{array}{r} 537 \\ +364 \\ \hline 901 \end{array}$$

doesn't your mind group the answer
into 9 hundreds, o tens, 1 unit?

When you have a system based on ten, you have to have
ten symbols.

The Hindus used symbols like this:

o ? ૨ ૩ 8 ૫ ౬ ౮ ౽ ౻

Through the years they have come to look like this:

0 1 2 3 4 5 6 7 8 9

When we are counting with these symbols, and we have
reached nine, how do we use them to show higher numbers?

We move the 1 over to the ten place, and put a zero in the
unit place.

10 11 12 13 14 15 16 17 18 19

and again, with the next number,

20 21 22 23 24 25 26 27 28 29

What would you do if you had a system based on twelve?
First, you would have to have twelve different symbols:

0 1 2 3 4 5 6 7 8 9 t e

Now, what would you do when you wanted to show a
number higher than eleven?

The same thing you do when you get back to base in
our own system, of course!

0 1 2 3 4 5 6 7 8 9 t e 10

a system based on twelve numerals would look like this

But you say "1" followed by "0" is "10"? You're right! Except that now that numeral (let's call it "one-zero") would stand for this many things:

Could you make up a numeration system using *any* number as a base?

Well, you couldn't have a system that used only one numeral, because that isn't enough to work with. But you can make up a system based on any number more than one.

what could you do with only 1 numeral?

You just have to remember that when you have used up all the symbols in your new system you start with the first one again, but you move it over one place.

if you had a base of two numerals, including zero, it would look like this   0 1 10   and one-zero would stand for this many things

If you had a base of six and used six numerals (including zero) it would look like this:

O   1   2   3   4   5
10 11 12 13 14 15

Now, one-zero would stand for this many things and one-one would stand for 1 more than that.

26

It's like learning a new language. When you're used to calling a four-legged animal that looks like this

a cow,

it's very hard when someone suggests you start calling it a horse.

But if you had always called it a horse, and you had always called this animal

a cow,

and everyone else did the same thing, then there would be no problem.

It's good practice to try thinking about things in a different way than you ever have before.

Try thinking about one-zero standing for this many objects:

or this many:

Can you feel your mind stretching a little?

THE BINARY SYSTEM
AND COMPUTERS

Almost 5,000 years ago, the Chinese seemed to have known about a numeration system based on two numerals. Somehow people forgot all about this system until a famous mathematician named Leibnitz began using it again. About 1700 A.D., he made a system using only 1 and 0.

But even Leibnitz did not realize how much this *binary* (which means "two-numeral") system would be used.

Now that you know how to build a numeration system, this one shouldn't be too hard to understand.

Remember, the binary system has a base of two. It uses only two numerals: "1" and "0."

Can you see how it works? Just as in the decimal system, every time a symbol is shifted one place to the left, its value is multiplied by the base.

So if two is the base,

4	which is	2×2	is written	100
8		$2 \times 2 \times 2$	is written	1000
16		$2 \times 2 \times 2 \times 2$	is written	10000

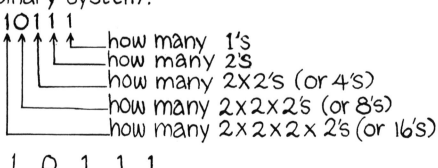

to write 23 in the binary system:

10111

     how many 1's
     how many 2's
     how many 2×2's (or 4's)
     how many 2×2×2's (or 8's)
     how many 2×2×2×2's (or 16's)

1   0   1   1   1

16 + 0 + 4 + 2 + 1 = 23

Isn't this the same thing we do in the decimal system?

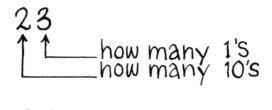

To Leibnitz, the binary system was mysterious and exciting. God, he said, was unity or *one*. And God created the whole world from emptiness, or *zero*. So he thought the two figures together, one and zero, could stand for everything in the universe.

Today, the binary system is one of the marvels of our world, but not at all in the way Leibnitz thought it would be. It is the system used by electronic digital computers. Sometimes we call them "electronic brains."

Some computers can add 40,000 complicated numbers in one second. Some computers can do problems in less than a minute that would take a mathematician, working eight hours a day, two weeks to solve. Since a computer works so fast, it doesn't matter that in the binary system 1 000 000 (one million)

is written

11110100001001000000

A computer can write that figure in 1/400,000th of a second.

A computer is a machine worked by electricity which can add, subtract, multiply, and divide, just as you can. But instead of having brains, it has thousands of electronic parts which either let electric current through or stop it.

When the current is on, that is 1 to the computer.

When the current is off, that is 0.

Can you imagine a new kind of traffic signal where the green light shining means GO, but no light means STOP?

Can you imagine somebody who says YES when he wants what you have, but says nothing when he doesn't want it?

That's the way a digital computer works.

Current on means GO or YES or 1.

Current off means STOP or NO or 0.

A computer can do long and complicated and difficult problems—problems no one has ever worked all the way through before. But a computer cannot work by itself. A mathematician must write out, in every detail, the problem he wants the computer to answer. Then he must "program" it, which means that he puts all the information on a tape the computer can "read" when it is put into the machine.

Holes are punched in the tape where the mathematician wants the computer to read "1," so the current can go through the holes.

Where he wants the machine to read "0", he doesn't punch a hole, and no current goes through. The computer has all the facts it needs stored in its "memory." When the tape is put in, it can solve the problem.

It's fun to imagine computers talking back and acting like people, but they are only machines that do arithmetic using the binary system. It is the men who think of the machines, and design them, and build them and use them who are the wonders. Just as the men who invented names for numbers, and the men who thought of zero are the amazing ones.

HOW MANY NUMBERS ARE THERE?

What is the biggest number you can think of?

A million?

A trillion?

A billion billion?

The words begin to sound like baby talk or nonsense, but there are such numbers and even bigger ones. They are hard to think about though, because unless we are scientists or mathematicians, we're not used to using such large numbers. Even the number 1 000 000 is difficult for us to picture.

What do a million pennies look like? Do you have any idea whether a pile of pennies that large would fill a basket or a bathtub or a room?

Well, if you counted them one at a time, at a normal speed, and didn't stop to eat or sleep or even sneeze, it would take 11 days and 14 hours of non-stop counting to reach 1 000 000.

But eventually you would get there, because there is such a number.

In fact, if a man had started to count when number systems began, and his oldest child continued counting when he died, and then *his* oldest child kept on counting, and this kept up through the centuries until this very minute, the person who was counting now would not have come to the end of numbers.

The number he would be up to now would be *smaller* than the numbers which scientists use every day. After all, the nearest star is almost 50 *trillion* miles away, and scientists have measured stars much farther away than that.

Scientists have been able to count the number of grains of sand on a beach. (About 1 with 20 zeros after it.)

They have been able to count the number of words that have been printed since the printing press was invented. (About 1 with 16 zeros after it.)

They have even been able to figure (approximately, of course) the number of words that have been spoken by people all over the world since the time cave men first grunted sounds. (About 1 with 16 zeros after it, or 10 million billion.)

They have learned that the number of atoms of oxygen in a thimble is greater than the number of grains of sand or printed words or spoken words. (About 1 with 27 zeros after it.)

1000000000000000000000000000

How can they do all this? Don't they get mixed up with all those zeros? And if it takes so long to count 1 000 000 pennies, don't scientists use up most of their time just writing down those huge numbers?

It would certainly be inconvenient to write those numbers out. Just one billion, which isn't very much as numbers go, looks like this: 1 000 000 000. But there is a kind of mathematical shorthand that makes things much easier.

Let's start with our old base, 10

If we multiply 10×10 we get one hundred.

But instead of writing out $10 \times 10 = 100$, we show that we are multiplying two tens this way:

$$10^2 = 100$$

Then instead of writing $10 \times 10 \times 10 = 1000$

we can write $10^3 = 1000$

The little number by the 10 is called an *exponent*.

Have you noticed two interesting things about it?

It tells how many times we have used 10 in the multiplication part. And it tells us how many zeros are in the answer. We don't have to write the answer at all.

How would you write one billion, which is a 1 with nine zeros after it?

You would write it 10^9.

The grains of sand on the beach would be 10^{20}.

And the oxygen atoms in the thimble would be 10^{27}.

10^{20} grains of sand

10^{27} atoms of oxygen

Simple, isn't it? You don't need fancy words like quintillion or sextillion. You just need the exponent. You don't even have to do the multiplication!

We call the answer a *power*.

Ten to the ninth power: 10^9

Ten to the twentieth power: 10^{20}

Ten to the twenty-seventh power: 10^{27}

There is a special name for one very large number, though. The number is 1 with a hundred zeros after it. A very famous mathematician named Dr. Kasner asked his nine-year-old nephew to think of a name for that number.

"I think we should call it a *googol*," the boy said. And that's what it is called today. The numeral 1 with a hundred zeros after it is a "googol." The same boy thought up a name for an even larger number; 1 with a googol of zeros after it. He called that a *googolplex*.

A "googolplex" is so big, that if you started writing it where you are and went around the earth—and not to the nearest but to the farthest star—you would not have enough room to write it.

a googolplex is
a number bigger
than all the
things there are

But still, it would be an actual number.

Then what is the biggest number?

Nobody knows. No matter how many numbers you count, you can always go on to the next one. Numbers go on forever—to *infinity*.

Bigger than the Biggest, and More than the Most

Where does infinity begin?

You might say it depends on who you are. The Hottentots are an African tribe which can only count to 3. If you ask a Hottentot how many fingers he has, he will say, "Many," because he can't think of a number big enough to count all his fingers.

That might sound funny because 10 is a very small number to us. But suppose someone asked you how many raindrops fall in a year. Maybe you would say that the number was *infinite* because you couldn't possibly imagine counting all those raindrops.

does a Hottentot have infinite fingers?

are there an infinite number of raindrops?

But, of course, the number of raindrops wouldn't be infinite. If scientists can count grains of sand and atoms, they could certainly count raindrops, and your idea of infinite raindrops would probably be as funny to them as the Hottentot's idea of an infinite number of fingers is to you.

Very, very big, or very, very many does not mean "infinite."

Even the word "countless" does not mean "infinite." Sometimes we talk about countless grains of sand or countless drops of water, but what we really mean is that there are so many they would be very difficult to count. It would be hard to find a place to begin, and a way of putting them in order so we could think about one number for each grain of sand or drop of water.

But they *could* be counted, because there is a definite number of grains of sand and a definite number of drops of water, even though you don't know what that number is.

"Infinite" means "without end."

Infinite things go on and on and on, forever.

Is it hard for you to imagine anything that doesn't end somewhere or sometime or somehow?

In a way, infinity is easier to imagine than some of the very big numbers, like a googolplex. It's just bigger or wider or higher or longer or more than anything anyone *can* imagine!

That's a giant step to take. But once you've taken it, the next time it isn't nearly so hard.

Do you get a strange feeling, thinking about infinity? Most people do, whether it is an infinity of numbers, or an infinity of space, or any other kind of infinity.

How many infinite things can you think of? (There are an infinite number of them!)

Numbers are infinite. You can always go on to the next one. Nobody can imagine an end to numbers. But even if they can't imagine an end, mathematicians *can* imagine more than one kind of infinite number, and they even work problems with them.

Here is the symbol for one kind of infinite number: $\aleph_0$ It is called "aleph-null."

It is not infinity itself, which is written like this: ∞

Could you work problems, using $\aleph_0$ or any of the other infinite numbers. Yes, you could, if you are prepared for some queer answers!

$$\aleph_0 + 3 = ? \quad \aleph_0 - 1492 = ? \quad \aleph_0 \times \text{googol} = ?$$

Did you get $\aleph_0$ as the answer to all the problems? If you think a minute, you'll see why it is the only possible answer.

Some queer things happen when you work with infinite numbers.

Wouldn't you say that there are twice as many numbers, odd and even together, as there are odd numbers, or even numbers?

After all, only half the numbers are odd numbers, and only half are even numbers, aren't they?

But look at this:

1 2 3 4 5 6 7 8 9 10 11 12 13 14 15 ...
2 4 6 8 10 12 14 16 18 20 22 24 26 28 30 ....

If you extended the top row of *all* the numbers to infinity— and extended the bottom row of only even numbers along with it, there would *always* be an even number in the bottom row to match the number in the top row.

So, all the way to infinity, the part of numbers that is the even numbers is equal to all the numbers together. Did you ever think that part of anything could be as much as the whole thing? Infinity is very strange.

Smaller than the Smallest, and Less than the Least

When we talk about infinite things, we usually mean infinitely large. But things can be infinitely small, too.

One is a small number. But we could divide it in half, and then divide it again and again and again into smaller and smaller fractions, and never reach the end. The fractions could go on and on forever, until they were *infinitesimal*, which means "infinitely small."

$$1 \quad \frac{1}{2} \quad \frac{1}{4} \quad \frac{1}{8} \quad \frac{1}{16} \quad \frac{1}{32} \quad \frac{1}{64} \quad \frac{1}{128} \quad \frac{1}{256} \quad \frac{1}{512} \quad \frac{1}{1024} \quad \frac{1}{2048} \quad \cdots$$

you could never come to the end

Sometimes we use this word when we talk about *things*. The smallest living things that can be seen under a microscope are bacteria, but you know that they aren't the smallest things in the world. Like everything else, they are made of molecules, and there are hundreds of millions of molecules in the smallest bacteria.

Molecules are so small that they are invisible under the most powerful microscopes, but they are huge compared to atoms. A molecule is a thousand times bigger than an atom of hydrogen.

each of these bacteria is only about $\frac{1}{25,400}$ th of an inch across

BUT bacteria are huge compared to molecules, which may be only $\frac{1}{100,000,000}$ th of an inch across

BUT molecules are bigger than atoms and an atom can be a trillion times bigger than its nucleus

And if you have ever been interested in atoms, you know that they are mostly empty space with electrons moving through them, around a center called a nucleus. A nucleus is about one trillionth the size of an atom.

If you think of bacteria,
then a molecule,
then an atom,
then a nucleus,

• nucleus

you are getting to something very, very small. Yet it isn't infinitely small. You can imagine it, and scientists have measured it. There are numbers much, much smaller. It's just about as difficult to take the step from very small to infinitesimal, as it is to take the step from very big to infinite.

SPECIAL NUMBERS

Do you think that 13 is an unlucky number? So many people do that most hotels do not even mark the thirteenth floor. Their floor numbers go from 12 to 14.

Do you have a lucky number? Can a number bring good or bad luck? Almost since the beginning of numbers, people have been fascinated by this idea. They have thought that certain numbers were good or bad. They have thought that some numbers were magic. They have even prayed to numbers.

The ancient Chinese thought that odd numbers, like 3 and 5 and 7, were male and that even numbers, like 2 and 4 and 6, were female. They thought some numbers stood for health, and some for special colors, and some for love.

The ancient Greeks spent a lot of time learning about numbers. They thought about them in two ways: Calculating, or counting, was something that common ordinary people like shopkeepers or fishermen had to do. But the study of numbers themselves—*that* was different! To study numbers you had to be a gentleman who did not need to work, and a person who was interested in strange and wonderful things.

The Greeks learned some strange and wonderful things about numbers.

Perfect Numbers

One of the things they enjoyed was the study of *perfect numbers.*

To find a perfect number, you list all the divisors of a number. Then you add the divisors. If they add up to the number you started with, then you have a perfect number.

6 is the first perfect number.

It can be divided by **1 2 3**

and **1 + 2 + 3 = 6**

The next perfect number the Greeks learned is 28. It can be divided by 1, by 2, by 4, by 7 and by 14. Add them together, and what is your answer?

$$1+2+4+7+14=28$$

The third and fourth perfect numbers took a long time to find. They are 496 and 8128. Have you noticed an interesting thing about perfect numbers? There is only one perfect number for the single digits—6. There is only one perfect number for the two-digit numbers—28. There is only one for the three-digit numbers—496, and one for the four-digit numbers—8128. And that's the way it goes.

It took 1,500 years to find the next perfect number, 33,-550,336. Up to now, only 17 perfect numbers have been discovered. The last one has 1,373 digits in it, and takes more than half a page to write!

While the Greeks were looking for perfect numbers, they found two other kinds—*redundant* and *defective.*

Redundant numbers have divisors which add up to *more* than the number itself.

18 is a redundant number. It can be divided by 1, 2, 3, 6 and 9. $1 + 2 + 3 + 6 + 9 = 21$, which is more than 18. So the Greeks said the divisors added up to too much. Maybe you can find some redundant numbers yourself.

Defective means *not complete,* so you can probably guess what a defective number is. Its divisors add up to *less* than the number.

16 is a defective number. It can be divided by 1, 2, 4, and 8. $1 + 2 + 4 + 8 = 15$, which is less than 16. Can you find some more defective numbers?

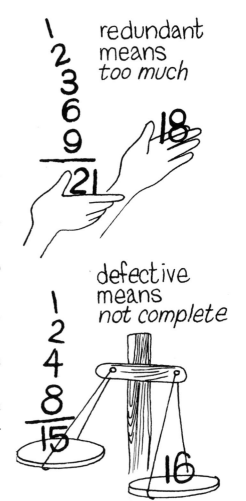

redundant means *too much*

defective means *not complete*

Prime Numbers

Another kind of number the Greeks enjoyed is called a *prime* number. *Prime* means *first.* A prime number cannot be divided by any number except 1 and itself.

2 is a prime number.

3 is a prime number.

Is 4 prime? No. It can be divided by 2.

5 is a prime number,

but 6 can be divided by 2 and 3.

7 is a prime number,

but 8, 9, and 10 are not.

11 is prime.

the first school you went to was *primary* school

41

the *sieve of Eratosthenes* is a quick
way of finding prime numbers

write the whole numbers, starting with the first prime, 2

2 3 4̶ 5 6̶ 7 8̶ 9̶ 1̶0̶ 11 1̶2̶ 13 1̶4̶ 1̶5̶ 1̶6̶ 17
1̶8̶ 19 2̶0̶ 2̶1̶ 2̶2̶ 23 2̶4̶ 2̶5̶ 2̶6̶ 2̶7̶ 2̶8̶ 29 3̶0̶ ..

after 2, cross out every *second* number. The first
number left is a prime, 3. Now cross out every *third*
number left. 5 is the next prime. Now cross out every
multiple of 5. what is 7 ? Can you find the next prim

How many prime numbers can you find up to 100? What
interesting thing do you see about all the prime numbers
larger than 2?

Numbers by Shape

The Greeks delighted in arranging numbers according to
the shapes they could make. This was not only fun, but
gave them useful information about the numbers.

One kind of number which you will use a great deal when
you study geometry is a *square* number.

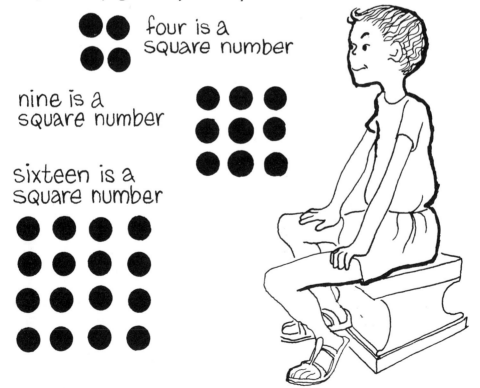

four is a
square number

nine is a
square number

sixteen is a
square number

What do you notice about square numbers?

The number on any one side is the same as the number on any other side. If you multiply the number on any one side by itself, the answer tells you the number of things in the square.

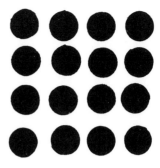

Do you remember one way we wrote

$$4 \times 4 = 16$$

$$10^2 = 100$$

We can do the same thing with any number.

$$4^2 = 16 \qquad 3^2 = 9 \qquad 2^2 = 4$$

The answer to any number multiplied by itself is a square number. So instead of saying we are using 10 to the second power, or 4 to the second power, we can say 10 *squared* or 4 *squared*. It seems funny to have that little ² mean "squared," but we're getting used to having odd things happen with numbers.

The Greeks also found *triangle* numbers, like

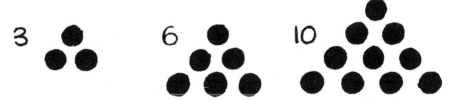

(Did you think the next one was going to be 9?)

To get the next triangular number you just add a bottom line one number bigger than the bottom line of the last triangle. What's the next one?

The Greeks also found rectangle numbers and pyramid numbers and cube numbers. Can you figure out what any of them are? Some, like square and rectangle numbers, are flat, like this page. Some, like cube numbers, have depth, like a box.

to get a square number

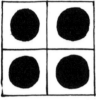

$2 \times 2 = 4$

you have only 2 numbers to multiply

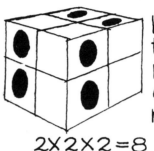

but you have to multiply 3 numbers to get a cube number.

$2 \times 2 \times 2 = 8$

Negative Numbers

Have you ever heard of negative numbers? *Negative* means "not." How can you have a *not number*?

You have to have less than zero to have a negative number.

How is that possible? Can you have less than no apples? Can there be less than no water in your glass?

what does a no apple look like?

how would you describe less than no water?

When it comes to apples and water and other things you can touch and hold, of course it isn't possible. But in the world of numbers, less than zero is used all the time.

44

A minus sign before a number shows that it is that much less than zero.

You have to go through zero to get to the negative numbers. Zero holds its own place as a divider between + and −

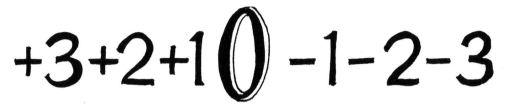

+3 +2 +1 0 −1 −2 −3

Sometimes you count backward, up to zero.

If zero is the time for a rocket launching, they say:

Zero minus 3

Zero minus 2

Zero minus 1

FIRE!

and that's zero.

Sometimes you can count down from zero.

If the temperature is terribly cold, we say the thermometer is below zero, and the temperatures might look like this:

Ten below zero is written −10°

(° means "degrees")

Twenty-three below zero −23°

Forty-five below zero   −45°

Negative numbers are useful in many ways.

On a map, sea level is 0. A mountain 1,520 feet high is 1,520 feet above sea level. But there are places like Holland or Death Valley that are below sea level. So, on maps you will see their elevations (or heights) written like this: −15, or −50 feet, or whatever they are below sea level.

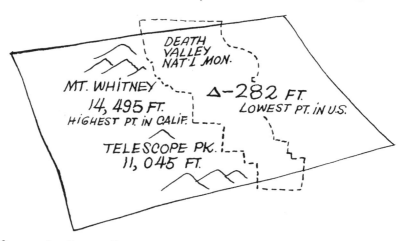

If you look at the dashboard of a car you will see a dial that shows + when the generator is charging, and − when the generator is discharging. In between is 0.

Sometimes negative numbers are written to the right of zero, like this:
or below it, like this:

0 −1 −2 − 3 − 4

But you must always go through zero to the other side (the way Alice went through the looking-glass) to come to the negative numbers.

Other Kinds of Numbers

We could go on and on, (but not to infinity!) talking about kinds of numbers. Some of them you know, like fractions and decimal numbers. Some day you'll learn about some of the others:
imaginary numbers,
rational numbers,

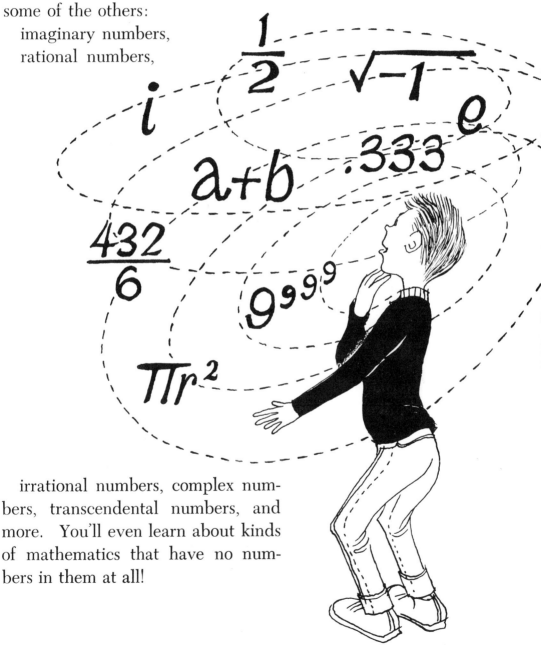

irrational numbers, complex numbers, transcendental numbers, and more. You'll even learn about kinds of mathematics that have no numbers in them at all!

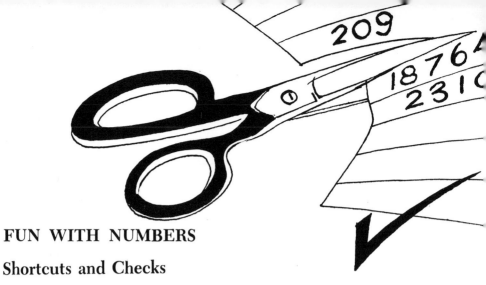

FUN WITH NUMBERS

Shortcuts and Checks

The Greeks thought that only "arithmetica," the study of numbers, was interesting and worth studying. Counting was something you had to do if you didn't have servants to do it for you. But through the years, people have found the counting part interesting, too. They have learned all sorts of tricks in addition, subtraction, multiplication, and division.

Maybe some of these will help you! Of course, there are mathematical reasons for all these shortcuts. Whole books have been written just to explain them.

Casting Out Nines

This is a way of checking addition that used to be taught to school children all the time. Then teachers decided that since it was not an *absolutely* perfect way of checking, they would not use it any more. But it is fun to do, once you know how, and you can generally depend on it.

Suppose you want to check the following problem:

First, add each row across, dropping out the 9's as you go, like this: In the first row, 534, you can see that 5 and 4 make 9, and all that is left is 3. So in a separate column, write 3.

$$
\begin{array}{r}
534 \\
721 \\
981 \\
787 \\
430 \\
\hline
3453
\end{array}
$$

The first three numbers will look like this:

534	3
721	1
981	O

(because $7 + 2 = 9$)
(you drop the 9, and $8 + 1 = 9$)

What about the next line, **787** ?

$7 + 8 = 15$, drop 9, which leaves 6. Then add that 6 to the 7. $6 + 7 = 13$, drop 9, leaving 4.

Now your problem looks like this:

534	3
721	1
981	O
787	4
430	7
3453	15

The last step is to cast the 9's out of the answers, so

$$6 = 6$$

Right? Right!

Let's try one more:

630	O
754	7
326	2
985	4
273	3
2968	16

$$7 = 7$$

Didn't this one go much faster? You could just about do it as you looked at it.

You can use this system of casting out nines to check multiplication, too. All you have to do is cast the nines out of the numbers that are being multiplied, and out of the answers, like this:

cast the 9's out of these numbers $\quad$ 637 $\quad$ which leaves $\quad$ 7

$$\begin{array}{r} 637 \\ \times\ 134 \\ \hline 2548 \\ 1911 \\ 637 \\ \hline \end{array}$$

$$\begin{array}{r} 7 \\ \times\ 8 \\ \hline 56 \end{array}$$

and out of the answers, which leaves $\qquad$ 85358

$$2 \qquad = \qquad 2$$

Shortcuts in Multiplication

Of course, multiplying by 10 or 100 or 1000 is easy. All you have to do is write down the number you are multiplying and add the number of zeros in the multiplier. (Remember place value?)

$$\begin{array}{r} 6285 \\ \times\ \ \ 10 \\ \hline 62,850 \end{array} \qquad \begin{array}{r} 3750 \\ \times\ \ 100 \\ \hline 375,000 \end{array} \qquad \begin{array}{r} 7495 \\ \times\ 1000 \\ \hline 7,495,000 \end{array}$$

It is almost as easy to multiply by 30 or 400 or 5000, because you only have to multiply by the first digit and then add the zeros. Although you almost always put numbers in their proper columns (10's in the 10 column, 100's in the 100 column), this is one time when it is easier not to do that. If you push them to one side, it makes the multiplying easier.

$$\begin{array}{r} 72 \\ \times\ \ 30 \\ \hline 2160 \end{array} \qquad \begin{array}{r} 836 \\ \times\ \ \ \ 400 \\ \hline 334400 \end{array} \qquad \begin{array}{r} 3413 \\ \times\ \ \ \ \ 5000 \\ \hline 17065000 \end{array}$$

Complementary Multiplication

This shortcut to multiplication is a little more complicated, but it is based on the same principle of multiplying by 100.

Suppose you had to multiply two numbers that were both a little less than 100, say 96 × 92.

How much does each number need to make it 100? That number is called its *complement*.

$$\begin{array}{r} 96 \\ \times\ 92 \\ \hline \end{array}$$
4 (complement because 96 + 4 = 100)
8 (complement because 92 + 8 = 100)

Now, from 96 subtract 8, the complement of 92.

This gives you 88, and those are the first two numbers in the answer. Then multiply the two complements 4 × 8 = 32. Those are the last two numbers in your answer.

$$\begin{array}{r} 96 \\ \times\ 92 \\ \hline 8832 \end{array}$$

$$\begin{array}{cc} 96 & 4 \\ -\ 8 & \times 8 \\ \hline 88 & 32 \end{array}$$

Try another one:

$$\begin{array}{r} 95 \\ \times\ 91 \\ \hline \end{array}$$
5 (complement)
9 (complement)

From 95 subtract the other complement, 9, which gives you the first two numbers in the answer, 86. Then multiply the complements, which make 45.

The answer should be 8,645, but let's do the whole problem and see:

$$\begin{array}{r} 95 \\ \times\ 91 \\ \hline 95 \\ 855\ \\ \hline 8645 \end{array}$$

it works!

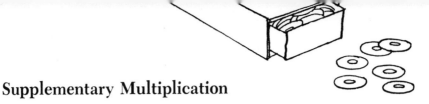

Supplementary Multiplication

If a number is a little more than 100, you can do something *similar*, which means *nearly the same*. The amount that each number goes over 100 is its *supplement*.

$$\begin{array}{r} 115 \\ \times 103 \end{array}$$ 15 (supplement because $15 + 100 = 115$)
3 (supplement because $3 + 100 = 103$)

To 115 *add* 3, the supplement of the other number.
So the first numbers in your answer should be 118.
Then multiply the supplements. The last numbers should be 45. The answer is 11,845. Work out the problem the long way and see if that's right.

Let's try one more:

$$\begin{array}{r} 112 \\ \times 106 \\ \hline 672 \\ 000 \\ 112 \\ \hline 11872 \end{array}$$ 12 (supplement)
6 (supplement)

$112 + 6 = 118$
$12 \times 6 = 72$

answer: 11872
right again!

Remember, if the numbers are *less* than 100, you subtract the complement. If they are *more* than 100, you *add* the supplement. That's all there is to it.

Multiplying by 11

Suppose you want to multiply $$\begin{array}{r} 245 \\ \times 11 \end{array}$$

First write down the right-hand digit, 5.
Then, going from *right to left*, add the first two digits there, 5 and 4, and write down 9.
Then add the last two digits, 4 and 2, and write down the answer, 6.

Then write down the end digit, 2.

The answer should be 2,695. Is it?

Remember, you always work from right to left.

$$245 \qquad 5$$
$$\text{then } 5+4 \qquad 95$$
$$\text{then } 4+2 \qquad 695$$
$$\text{write the first number } 2695$$

Sometimes you have to carry when you are adding the digits. Add the number you carry to the sum of the next pair of digits, like this:

$$958 \times 11 = 10{,}538$$

Write down the 8.

Then $8+5=13$. Write down the 3 and carry the 1.

$5+9=14$ and the 1 you carried makes 15. Write down the 5 and carry the 1.

Write down the end digit. But you have carried 1, so that changes the 9 to 10.

$$8$$
$$38$$
$$538$$

answer:

$$10538$$

Work this one out the fast way, and see if you get the same answer.

Multiplying by 50

This is easy. Add two zeros to the number you are multiplying and divide by 2.

Multiplying by 25

Easy, too. Add two zeros and divide by 4.

$$3692 \times 25 = 4\overline{)369200} = 92300$$

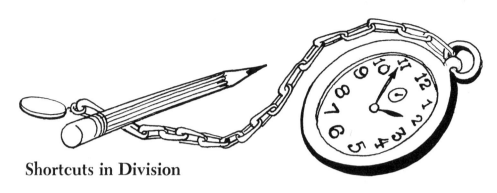

Shortcuts in Division

Can you tell by looking at a number whether it can be divided exactly by another number? Do you know if 5,464 can be divided by 8, with nothing left over? Or whether 79,084 can be divided by 7, with nothing left over?

These rules will help you find out:

test for dividing

by 2 A number can be divided by 2 if the end digit on the right side is even. (2, 4, 6, 8, 0)

by 3 A number can be divided by 3 if you add all the digits in the number and the *sum* can be divided by 3. (In 2358, $2 + 3 + 5 + 8 = 18$, 18 can be divided by 3, so 2,358 can be divided by three.)

by 4 A number can be divided by 4 if the last 2 right-hand digits can be divided by 4. (97,624 can be divided by 4 because 24 can be divided by 4.)

by 5 A number can be divided by 5 if it ends in 5 or 0.

by 6 A number can be divided by 6 if it is even, and the sum of its digits can be divided by 3.

by 7 No one has found an easy test for this. Maybe you can!

by 8 A number usually can be divided by 8 if the sum of the last three digits can be divided by 8, or if the last three digits are zeros.

by 9 A number can be divided by 9 if the sum of its digits can be divided by 9.

54

Mathematical Shorthand

Another way to do numbers faster is to make symbols stand for things that take longer to write out. We have already used some of them:

    ∞   stands for infinity

    2   stands for multiplying a number by itself, or squaring it

    °   stands for degrees ($-26°$)

Of course these signs,

$$+ \text{ for } add,$$
$$\text{and } - \text{ for } subtract,$$

are mathematical shorthand too.

There are several ways of saying *divide*.

    ⌐   is one, and ÷ is another.

When you write fractions, like ½, the line between the one and the 2 means "divide." You are saying 1 divided by 2.

There are several ways of writing *multiply*.

✕ is one way.

But in algebra and geometry, people use the letters x and y and z, and many others, so ✕ for "multiply" would be confusing. Sometimes they put a dot between the numbers to say "multiply."

$$10 \cdot 10 \cdot 10 = 1000$$

Sometimes they use parentheses   4(8) to say "multiply."

Here are some other symbols in mathematical shorthand. They are used mostly in algebra and geometry, but nobody says they can't be used in other kinds of number work. Some people even use these signs when they want to write English quickly.

∴ means "therefore"   < means "is less than"

> means "is greater than"   ∼ means "is similar to"

Puzzles and Challenges

Many of our games, like dominoes, or parchesi, or roulette are actually number games. But there are special ways of playing with the numbers themselves that are so entertaining you might play for hours or days or months, just arranging and rearranging numbers.

Magic Squares

There is nothing really magic about magic squares, although once people gave all sorts of meanings to them. They substituted letters for the numbers (A for 1, B for 2, and so on) and proved, (they thought) that an event in the Bible was true, or that someone they knew was a real friend or enemy.

Although magic squares did teach us a great deal about how numbers are related to each other, today we use them mostly for fun.

The earliest magic square we know about is almost 3,000 years old. If we use Arabic numbers instead of the original Chinese, it looks like this:

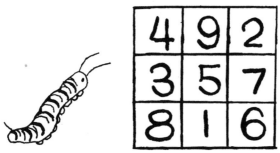

4	9	2
3	5	7
8	1	6

Any way you add the columns, the answer is 15, whether you add the columns across, down, or even on the diagonal.

Perhaps the most famous magic square is in an engraving by the artist Albert Dürer. He made it in the year 1514, and the square was only a small part of the picture. But when people looked at the square carefully, this is what they saw:

Like other magic squares, all the rows, columns, and diagonals add up to the same number—in this square it is 34. But this is an even more marvelous magic square.

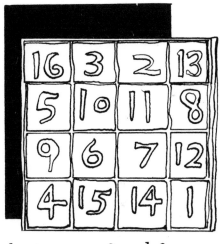

The four numbers in the corners add up to 34.

The four numbers in the center add up to 34.

The four numbers in each quarter add up to 34.

The two numbers in the middle of the top row, 3 and 2, and the two numbers in the middle of the bottom row, 15 and 14, add up to 34.

The two numbers in the middle of the first column, and the two numbers in the middle of the last column add up to 34.

Can you work out any more things with this one magic square? There are pages and pages of them! Can you make up a magic square of your own?

The "Fifteen" Puzzle

You have probably seen a little puzzle with movable numerals that looks like this:

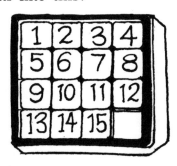

Less than a hundred years ago this puzzle was so popular in Europe that it was played in the streets, in royal palaces, in offices and factories, and even by statesmen and government officials.

Large sums of money were offered as prizes, but nobody ever won these prizes, even though the game looked so simple.

The game was invented by a man named Sam Lloyd.

He decided how the numbers were to be arranged in the box. Then newspapers all over Europe printed each puzzle, and everyone tried to arrange the numbers that way. Why couldn't they do it?

Well, two American mathematicians have proved that with the numbers in any given order, you can move them to about 10 *trillion* positions. But there are about 10 trillion *other* positions to which you cannot possibly move them.

Sam Lloyd must have been a very clever mathematician. The positions that he printed in the newspapers were always among the 10 trillion that were impossible! So his prize money was always safe.

Fibonacci Numbers

In the year 1202, Leonardo of Pisa, who was also known as Fibonacci, made up a fascinating series of numbers. They begin like this:

1, 1, 2, 3, 5, 8, 13, 21, 34, 55, 89, 144,

What a strange line of numbers!

They're not all odd.

They're not all even.

They're not arranged by 2's or 3's or 5's.

Before you look any further, see if you can figure out how they are arranged.

Each one is the sum of the two numbers just before it.

$$1 + 1 = 2$$
$$1 + 2 = 3$$
$$2 + 3 = 5$$
$$3 + 5 = 8$$
$$5 + 8 = 13$$
$$8 + 13 = 21$$

Can you go on after 144?

But this series of numbers is not just a test of how well you can add. There are some very strange and interesting things about it.

Let's write them in a column.

You can do an amazing trick with them.

Draw a line under any number. The sum of all the numbers above that line is equal to 1 less than the second number below it.

Draw a line under 8. The sum of all the numbers down to 8 is 20. The second number below the 8 is 21. Take away 1 and you have 20.

Try a line under 21. The sum of all the numbers down to 21 is 54, 1 less than the second number below the line.

Here's another trick.

Pick any three numbers that follow each other in line. Multiply the middle number by itself (square it). Then multiply the first number by the third number. The answer will always differ by 1.

Suppose you try 2, 3, and 5.

1
1
2
3
5
8
13
21
34
55
89
144

Scientists have learned that many things in nature work according to the Fibonacci series of numbers, even the distances between leaves on a plant!

Remarkable Nine

One of the most interesting of all numbers is 9.
Think of any number.   Make it as long as you like.

$$7\,6\,3\,2\,9\,8\,1\,6\,4\,7\,5\,0\,2\,8\,1$$

Now rearrange the digits any way you want to, to make another number.

$$1\,2\,8\,0\,7\,4\,6\,5\,1\,9\,8\,2\,3\,7\,6$$

Subtract the smaller number from the greater one.

$$
\begin{array}{r}
763298164750281 \\
-\ 128074651982376 \\
\hline
635222351276 7905 \\
\end{array}
$$

$$9\,)\,\overline{635222351276\,7905}$$
$$705803903075 45$$

The answer can *always* be divided by 9.

What is the largest number you can write, using only four digits? $9^{9^{9^9}}$

You can do some beautiful things with 9.

$$9 \times 9 + 7 = 88$$
$$98 \times 9 + 6 = 888$$
$$987 \times 9 + 5 = 8888$$
$$9876 \times 9 + 4 = 88888$$
$$98765 \times 9 + 3 = 888888$$
$$987654 \times 9 + 2 = 8888888$$
$$9876543 \times 9 + 1 = 88888888$$
$$98765432 \times 9 + 0 = 888888888$$

Here's another trick with 9's:

$$999999 \times 2 = 1999998$$
$$999999 \times 3 = 2999997$$
$$999999 \times 4 = 3999996$$
$$999999 \times 5 = 4999995$$
$$999999 \times 6 = 5999994$$
$$999999 \times 7 = 6999993$$
$$999999 \times 8 = 7999992$$
$$999999 \times 9 = 8999991$$

Here's another trick that uses the 9 table:
(But remember to *leave out* the 8's.)

$$12345679 \times 9 = 111111111$$
$$12345679 \times 18 = 222222222$$
$$12345679 \times 27 = 333333333$$
$$12345679 \times 36 = 444444444$$
$$12345679 \times 45 = 555555555$$
$$12345679 \times 54 = 666666666$$
$$12345679 \times 63 = 777777777$$
$$12345679 \times 72 = 888888888$$
$$12345679 \times 81 = 999999999$$

And have you ever taken a really good look at the 9 table?
The answers at both ends of the table, going toward the
middle, are the same numbers turned around!

$$2 \times 9 = 18$$
$$3 \times 9 = 27$$
$$4 \times 9 = 36$$
$$5 \times 9 = 45$$
$$6 \times 9 = 54$$
$$7 \times 9 = 63$$
$$8 \times 9 = 72$$
$$9 \times 9 = 81$$

WHO NEEDS NUMBERS?

Everybody!

Numbers are fun to play with, but we couldn't do without them in our everyday lives. And almost everybody who works at any kind of a job needs some kind of numbers.

For most jobs, you need more than one kind.

Everybody needs arithmetic.

Anyone who wants to solve a problem in which he has unknown numbers needs algebra.

If you want to be a carpenter or an architect, a navigator or a surveyor, you need geometry, and usually trigonometry, too.

And if you want to design cars or motors, be an engineer or a chemist, an astronomer or a physicist you have to study the calculus on top of all the others.

All of these kinds of mathematics are exciting. The more we know about numbers, and the more imagination we use, the more marvelous they become.

Because numbers + imagination = new ideas.

And new ideas are always exciting!

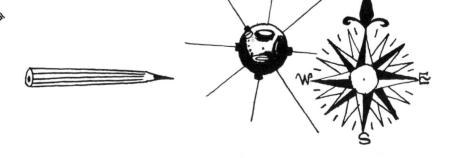

Index

About the Authors

JEANNE BENDICK has both written and illustrated a great number of books for young people, including many in the science field.

With her clear, concise writing, and her illustrative—and amusing—drawings, she is able to make even the most difficult subject simple and exciting.

Whittlesey House books that she has written and illustrated are: *How Much and How Many*, updated 1960; *Electronics for Young People*, New Fourth Edition; *What Could You See;* with her children, *Have a Happy Measle;* and with Robert Bendick, *Television Works Like This*, Third Revised Edition.

Mrs. Bendick lives in Rye, New York, with her husband and two children.

MARCIA O. LEVIN is the author of a number of books for very young children and of a book series for teen-age girls. *Take a Number* is her first Whittlesey House book. After studying at Philadelphia Normal School and Temple University, Mrs. Levin taught in the Philadelphia public schools for over eleven years. She now lives in Rye, New York, with her husband and three children.